You *ARE* your Spiritual Self...The Poetry Within

By

Joelle Mueller

United in Spirit,
Joelle Mueller

To Order
go to:
www.youareyourspirit.com
or call:
1-888-280-7715

ISBN: 1-4107-3597-4 (e-book)
ISBN: 1-4107-3596-6 (Paperback)

This book is printed on acid free paper.

Cover design and illustration by Stephanie Brueggemann. She can be reached at: mbruegge@comcast.net
Author portrait by Nancy Ryan. She can be reached at: nryanart@aol.com

1stBooks – rev. 04/12/03

This publication is not intended to treat or be a substitute for therapy or professional advice. It is offered with the understanding that the content expressed, herein, is the opinion of the author and neither the author nor the publisher is rendering medical or psychological service.

Dedication

With grateful appreciation

to all the teachers who have

passed through my life and

to those who have remained.

Acknowledgements

There are many people who have passed through my life and who are now in my life, who have helped shape who I am. I thank all of them.

I will focus, here, on a few, knowing those not specifically named, will understand and know they are included as well.

> ➢ Thank you, Creative Spirit, for open eyes and heart and for the awareness of Your warm love, passionate ideas, and constancy in my life.
>
> ➢ Thank you, John and JoAnn Mueller, for the gift of unconditional love. You have given this gift to me and demonstrated it to others. You both were the first of many blessings in my life. I love you Mom. I love you Dad.
>
> ➢ Thank you, Jody, for your unselfish support and your often goofy zest for life. God blessed us by bringing us together and blesses us still. I love you.

- Thank you, Michelle LeMier, for your long-time friendship and love.

- Thank you, Kathy Fick, for encouraging me not to give up on my spirituality when I felt religion giving up on me.

- Thank you, Shelley Moore, for showing me, in my formative years, that a little irreverence can be fun and needed at times, and also for showing me that it is okay to experience all the fun and joy there is to be had in life.

- Thank you, Donna Sousa, for introducing me to the concept that one person's thoughts can change the fate of the world. I thought you were crazy. Now, I know better.

Introduction

You flower like a tree as you awaken to your spiritual self. You carry radiantly colored blossoms and all is bright and good. Then, daily life happens and it seems as if your blossoms wilt and fall away from you as you become more and more immersed in deadlines, routine, dashed expectations, world affairs, and personal crises.

You may look at your bare branches and feel depressed or confused or even resentful toward Nature for once providing you with such beautiful reminders of Its presence with you, then leaving you to stand naked against the elements.

You may have many seasons of blossoming and wilting. Then, this year, you blossom and bear fruit. You realize Nature has provided you with enough spiritual nutrition that you now have a crop of spiritual food to share with everyone you encounter.

You may still have dormant seasons, but you *always* have the potential in you to produce more fruit. This is how you are built. Nature created you, a being, with all the structures, all the intelligence, all the soul, and all the natural know-how to be able to produce spiritual fruit. It is all there, all the time.

The point rests here: The enlightened guru and wise spiritual advisor that you may or may not be seeking, lie within you. They *are* you. That wisdom is the part of you that is intuition, that is stillness and calm when life is swirling around you. It is what you truly are. It is what you were before you had a body. That Wisdom is your essence. It is the spark, in you, from the Divine Fire that created you. Simply put, you *are* your Spiritual Self.

May Nature bless your blossomings

And make you prosperous in your seasons.

Joelle Mueller

March 2, 2003

x

Important Clarifications

It may be of benefit for you to know, these poems were written chronologically through the years. The first poem in this book is the first spiritually-intentioned poem I wrote, at the beginning of *my* conscious blossoming. They go on from there, in succession, to the last poem of the collection; the last poem before a new fruit-bearing season.

As you read (if you read in succession) you will notice the use of the words "I", "Me", "Mine", "My", "You", and various other capitalized pronouns. These capitalizations are used intentionally, to reference the Divine.

The following selections are meant for you to interpret in any way that fits for you. There is no "correct" or intended interpretation, except for the way in which your heart responds.

The Naked Journey

The wake rolls against you
as you paddle with naked toes
in the opposite direction…
    But you almost don't recognize
    your toe's strain,
because you were born in this water;
you belong in its wetness;
your toes were meant to dip into it;
your body was created to swim in it—
    through it—
to the mouth and delta and the open sea
of your ending and beginning.

Joelle Mueller

The Ripple Effect

Stick your head in the water
and move it around,
just looking for food,
and the ripples that go out
from your dunked head
affect the rock across from you,
the shoreline,
the sediment beneath you,
the fish swimming next to you,
the King Fisher diving from
Heaven to prey.
All is touched
by your active water rings—
to infinity
or to the end of your waterway.

Today Forever

Today I will know these moments
    and the moments that belong in
    the arms of the future.

Today I will walk the steps that have been
    sunk into the sand, by my own feet,
    when I was yet a light in Heaven.

Today I will speak the words I have grown
    to know as truth and whisper prayers
    to be shown greater truths that I
    may profess with every drawn breath.

Today I will pray for the courage
    to pray and the ability to listen
    when answered.

And today I pray for knowledge of
    Oneness…already within Your arms
    I still struggle to feel their warmth.

But today I light a candle;
    A connection, a flame of passion,
    a glow of faith, a flicker of the
    pulsing light within and around me.

Today I celebrate, for truly,
    it is the first day of the rest
    of my life.

Joelle Mueller

Wish I May

They used to say, a lost eyelash
blown from a fingertip
would find your wish.

They used to say "I wish I may"
on the first star of the evening sky
would grant the wish
of dreaming minds.

They teach that luck
is the fate of dreams; giving them
over to abstract themes that
help you hide your role
in grasping the dreams
when they drift, your whole life,
just out of reach.
And all you really need do
to make your dreams happen
is to make your dreams happen.

Possibility vs. Reality

Fires can burn,
trees can fall,
death can strike,
disease can prevail,
the wars can come,
    but
children will always be.
Water will always quench.
Smiles will always
be easier to make
and strangers will
always, only, be unmet friends.

Joelle Mueller

The Flower

The veins of the petals
bleed out to the edges
even before it has been
pressed between holy pages.

Its birth showed light
but developed dark veins
as it grew.

Its life, cut short
by the length of its stem,
withers and wilts,
its neck bent low,
'till it drops its petals
by the base of its source,

then lifted and saved
within holy places,
they never become dry,
the blood turns to wine
and their velvet is soft
through the pages of time.

On the Threshold

Standing on the edge of the mind,
like a suicidal jumper
is the mentality of this species;
trembling with nerves and fear,
fat with ideas of power and wealth
and manipulated by
notions of vengeance
disguised in robes as legal justice.

All twined up tight and safe inside,
without conscious questioning.
Then cowers on the edge
of the mind, just so,
when the truth of life evolves.
It needs to spring from the place
it squats, for it is afraid
of conscious Life.
It is too smart to take up arms
and too weak to battle Light.

Joelle Mueller

Dwelling On It

Squirrels skip along the top branches
through the sunlight dappled bark,
dropping the remains of their supper
for the grass dwellers.
    And one or two scramble desperately
    at the thin, bending ends
    of their branches,
    trying to get a foothold after venturing past
    the safe zone of thicker, older limbs.
But, after minutes, the scrambler finds its hold
and nimbly jogs down the trunk
to hunt for more nuts.
    Kudos to the risktaker; the scrambler.
    But, courage lost,
    I'm stayed in the grass;
    afraid the scramblers will knock me
    out of their tree.

Words Are Life

Words go together easily
when you know their rhythms.
They bond with each other
to form sonnets and songs.
Some rhyme and some clash
but, as in all life,
each connection made
lends greatness to the soul.

Joelle Mueller

Life Is

Tree bark looks dead
to those living a lie
but moss and ants and fungus
live the truth
in all its sides.

It seems
what appears to be dead
to one,
can breed
life in another
who gleans purpose and truth,
beyond only death;
perceived by the other.

Aspiring gods

The water just flows on
like its supposed to,
surging at the sands of ages
like the laws of physics demand;

while the most unnatural
thing is swirling,
dancing buoyant
with the tension of the surface.

The unnatural bodes toxic and evil
to the feeding duck, snails, and shore plants
then drops its hooks down deeper
tempting lakebed life to an end.

But the unnatural, too, is innocent;
Obeying only the nature of things;
merely coming to float there by consequence
of the imagined laws of aspiring gods.

They deny failed attempts at creation
while grasping for Ultimate power,
then empathize with public outcries
with words and withering flowers.

It is these gods
who think they are not bound
to the laws of earth and sky,
who are the most unnatural enemy
to all the lives of this time.

Joelle Mueller

Cool Hands

Everything in this life is hot
to one or another;
    Passionate hot.
Summer lovemaking in the vinyl back seat hot.
    We versus them hot.
    Him versus her hot.
    Ash-white cinder hot.
White knuckles on the wheel.
Fuck finger in the air hot.
    Morality versus truth.
    Politics versus justice.
    The individual versus all.
No one thing is neutral
in the hot head mind.
    Take a breath.
    Blow it across your brain.
Let the heat ebb and peace cool your mind.

Philosophy

I lie back
and devise a philosophy
with which
to build my life…
    with my two cats;
Gray rolled up in the corner
hiding her nose;
    the other
hunched on the closest
bed corner (freshly made);
her black bottlebrush bristles
standing at attention
to the neighbor's agitated dog.

What philosophy can I glean
from these two;
    one cowering,
    one cautious
and prepared to confront;
Gray allowing Black
to battle the throngs
and Black willing to do it;
willing to risk her self
for the noble cause of wisdom;
growing out of courage
in the face of fear.

Joelle Mueller

Persons

Some are fluidity,
    stuck
    in unchanging mire—
with the hearts
    of passion-filled artists
but with minds
    absent in knowledge
of brushes and oils
    and painting technique,
familiar with only the emotion
    desiring expression on canvas.
And, after attempts,
    are left with a colorful
rendering of knowledge's lack—

The emotion still
    stuck
    in the unchanging mire.

Like Perfect Weather

They are bright souls
settling into hearts of others
through serene eyes, grace-filled words,
genuine touch and gentle breath.

They are those who
glide into our everyday;
glowing warmth,
peace, confidence and love.

They enfold our spirits
and inspire our souls to trust.

Joelle Mueller

Tired?

What is "being tired"?
Is your body aching;
your eyelids drooping;
the eyeballs dry and sore?

Do your thoughts feel fuzzy;
your attention shift;
your breathing turn
to rumbling?

Is your body bent;
your eyes downcast;
your spirit bored with living?

Is your anger rising;
your passion waning;
your contentment drained away?

Turn your thoughts up;
hear that small voice;
perpetual, still, and warm.

And realize the power
you give up to your ego
then become wise to the lies it purports.

Put Into Words

All the enlightened ones
say, "Look inside yourself
to find God."

"God is within you."
"You are God."

Am I God? or
am I a piece of the collective whole of God;
a piece of the whole
of creation;
a piece just as the dog
or the cat
or the sky or a cactus.

Just a piece of the whole
as every object with living
energy is a part of the whole.

So many vague concepts to be
sorted through and developed.
Concepts I haven't even put
into words.

Joelle Mueller

Poetry

This is my meditation.
This is my peace.
This is my breathing
and necessary release.

This is my connection
with that outside of myself;
the turn my mind takes
to nurture my health.

This is my reflecting pond
where I am gifted to see,
not through the eyes of my ego
but the grand Mystery.

This is my prayer,
my living in faith
with the Spirit of all
Who redeems hearts by grace.

As it is

Poetry is the vein
of consciousness
by which I realize
connection to this Life.

All creation is poetic;
dripping with rhythm
and potential recognition
of metaphoric life truths.

Joelle Mueller

Failing Fear

"I have it within me",
I tell myself.
Than why am I
so afraid of failing
at the very thing in which
I most desire success?

It seems, when I
choose a task,
neutrally,
success comes easily
but when passion plays
in my heart and hands,
fear rises
and my will succumbs
with merely a beginning effort.

Too afraid of succeeding?
Or…
Too afraid of failing
in the task
that reflects me inwards,
that mirrors the truth of my soul?
Too afraid of failing my true self.

But, too,
isn't it impossible
to fail your soul
when the truth of your passion
lights your path?

Transition

Within the years of hurt and hurting,
Within the resentment and curled
      lips of anger,
Within the disappointment and crushed
      expectations,
Within the rejection and smoldering
      memories,
Within the ingrained mazes we walk through
      called patterns,
Within the pained eyes and damp cheeks,
Within the barren self and valleys of mood...
      Lie the learner and the learning.
      Lie the blessed and the blessing.
      Lie the awakened and the awakening.
      Lies opportunity.

Joelle Mueller

If in Relationship

We happen to meet
the one we are with,
by chance, or coincidence, maybe.
But, maybe, too
we choose our mate
without recognition of choice.

You say "If we choose,"
"I wouldn't choose her."
"She's much too much of a pain."
But, truly, you chose
the mate you did,
knowing from her you could learn…

about self and respect
and where you fail
in compassion and right thinking.
And should your mind change
and you choose again,
you'll have the same lessons revealed.

Until you choose
to learn where you are
and stay with the one you are with,
you will limbo around
the relationship world
and never reveal your bliss.

Untitled

Love your hardness
and your softness.
Embrace them both
and you accept yourself.

Joelle Mueller

I Am

I look out from its eyes
as windshields.
I pull the levers, push the pedals,
and rotate the knobs
to steer it
where I want it to go.

The fuel is Divine
and perpetual,
lubricating all parts in a bath;
keeping them clean
and working like clocks.

Its never-ending and ever-present
and It works with me to plan
the route and drive the machine.
I am more than this body.
I am more than these parts.
I am more.
I Am.

Today

Today is a day of reckonings.
Today is a day of beginning.
Today I walk out the door
a mouse
and return with the lion.
Today ends in victory.
Darkness ends in light.
Today is a day of reckoning.
Today dawns the light
of my sight.

Joelle Mueller

Try to Fly

Learning to fly.
Learning to fly.
Learning to fly.
Learning to fly.
I am a fledgling
Learning to fly;
Flying to learn.
All is well.

To Me

To me, its Truth
that walks along
on the heals
of humankind;
dogging the steps
of all who breathe;
latching onto soles
like chewed gum
trying to cement
the heal with each stride;
to slow the walker,
to ground the cruiser,
then stretches stringy
as the heal lifts off
and moves along.
But, once Truth has stuck
it forever sticks.
And when enough
gets stuck,
to the scuffed up sole,
the wearer must stop
and survey.
For, the build-up of Truth
on the sole of your shoe
may show,
in your path,
a New way.

Amen

Amen.
It is done.
Amen,
is faith working.
Amen.
It is ancient prayer.
Amen.
There is a reason
we say amen.
It is a trust
and a knowing
that God is at work.
Amen.
All cares are gone
and there is peace.
Amen.

Stepping Up

Step this way
Step that way
Step forward
and back.
So many steps
I could easily
lose track.

Too many worries
about doing it right.
Too many fears
blocking out Loving Light.

Reality is;
there are no strikes
or wrong steps;
only choices
made freely
by minds out of step.

But, if we are silent
and spend time
in our hearts,
our steps become guided;
our way clearly marked.

Joelle Mueller

Birthright

In peace and contemplation
I ponder the value of my life.
So much of the time
I'm awestruck that You
would spend the time and caring
to act in my existence.

With all the others
You have to help
You've also chosen me.
I thank my stars,
fold my hands,
listen in the quiet
and sit humbly at Your knee.

Lifetime Prayer

Now I lay me
down to sleep.
I pray the Lord
my soul to keep.
When in the morning
light I wake,
show me the path
of love to take*…

This is my lifetime
prayer, God.
Every moment.
In every conversation,
In the gloomy
and the rainy
and in the multiple
faces of challenge…
Show me the path
of love to take.
     Amen.

prayer my mother adapted and taught to me as a child.

Joelle Mueller

All

The lamp light shows
in a half-moon
on the wall;
barely noticed any minute
unless focused on.
Within you glows
that same half-moon
that is your wellspring of joy,
that is your Truth,
your motivation,
your intuition and inspiration,
that is God;
the half-moon glow
within you
that burns softly without scorching;
the passionate flow
of all good that,
unlike the lamp,
cannot be switched off.
It is innate and everlasting.
It is All.

Spiritual Life

live it to feel it.
Don't just preach it.
live it to feel it,
Don't just think it
or read it.
Don't keep it outside yourself.
Don't learn it from outside yourself.
Learn it in
and keep it in.
Next, feel it in
and you will know
the feeling of
the spiritual life.

Joelle Mueller

Priority One

Prioritize my perspective.
Help me see the truth
to my day;
see the day
not for what happens in it
but for what
is behind those happenings;
See love as every
motivation and result
of action
and every action
as witness to the
reality of Love…
Priority One.

Seek Action

Seek and you will find
the dawning of a new mind.
Don't seek by sitting
or reading or listening
or following.
Seek by doing.
Action defines purpose.
Purpose clears mind.

Joelle Mueller

How

How do I feel closer toYou?
How do I open myself up
inside to feel You?
What has to happen
for the separation to end?
I walk the steps of this daily life
not much different than before.
There has to be more.
Help.

More Silence

Spend more time with Me.
Be with Me in the stillness.
Create around you
the stillness of noise
you need to hear Me.
Don't fret over the static
in your brain
that distracts you from Me.
Turn off the environmental static
and your mind will follow.
Don't worry about
not being able to feel Me
or hear Me in your life.
I speak all ways
so that you can hear Me.
Be still and quiet often
and you will know My voice
and you will know My touch.
I fill you
as light fills a room.
To have the answers you seek,
simply…
Spend more time with Me.

Joelle Mueller

I Am as are you

I Am like the sun,
bathing tree bark
on a cloudy late afternoon.
I Am like the feelings
this sight inspires;
safety, serenity, contentment,
warmth in the midst of coldness,
encompassing, condition-less love
that knows no selectivity.
For indeed,
I *Am* the sun and the bark
and the clouds,
and I *Am* the feelings
I engender.
And so are you.

God as my Cat

An angel with black paws
and claws
is kneading my head
as I rest it
on her favorite pillow.

God bless my angel cat
with her wet nose
and drooly lip
that she buries in my hair
so close I can feel
her motor purr.

God bless my angel cat
who shows me love
when I have a hard time
showing love to myself.

God bless my angel cat.

Real Simple

Think ugly,
get ugly.

Think good,
get good.

Think love,
get love.

Simple.

Seal the Deal

You have, within you,
the power to attain your dreams.
But you must not be afraid
to dream them.
Then you must not be afraid
to act on them,
for I Am the director
behind your soul.
If I Am for you,
who or what can be
against you.
Seal the deal.
Pray.

Joelle Mueller

Omnipotent me

Reflecting in the mirror
is the form
I think I know so well;
yet, not even I know
how many hairs
are on my head.

I think I know so well
the direction
my life is going
and the direction
my life will take;
yet, not even I know
when this life will end.

I think I know so well
that I have
friends and family who support;
yet, not even I know
when angels circle about.

I think I know so well;
yet, not even I know
what I think.

Know

Be strong in your way.
Know the truth in Me,
and know it as yourself.
Ask not what
the next step will be;
rather, just take it
and know it is intended.
For, you are the light
that shines for Me,
and I Am the light
which shines in you.
Be strong in your heart's way
and know I believe in you
and illuminate your way.

Memory

Why do I not feel like writing tonight?
Because I feel at peace from within?
Because I feel uncertain within?
- How to know, for certain, my calling?
- How to remain still and calm within?
- How not to grasp at every straw
  that floats by when, some days,
  I feel as if I were drowning?
My memory says "breathe" and "center"
and know confidence in the uncertainty.

You are where you are because
that's where you've chosen to be
to meet the need within.

Perplexed

My intellect proclaims;
all prosperity is mine.
The doors to the Universe
of prosperity are flung wide open
and wait for me to walk through.
But my eyes see glass doors,
not flung open, but stuck closed;
clear so as to see the other side
but, solid, too; preventing my passing through.
And so, I live in a state of perplexion
behind glass doors; tempted of possibility
but stayed by imagined boundary.

Joelle Mueller

Thank you

Thank you rests on my lips
frequently these days;
such a small phrase
that carries with it
life-enhancing properties.
Think "thank you",
Write "Thank you",
Say "Thank you",
and you will receive
all and more of
that for which
you are grateful.

Impossible

Well-intentioned
and strong of heart
we certainly still
get distracted...

Distracted from Truth
and harmonious living,
distracted from thinking
good thoughts.

To quiet the mind
seems near to
impossible,

but impossible exists
only in
our thoughts.

Joelle Mueller

Don't be Swayed

Let the seas roll outside of you,
as you are immersed
in the middle of the waves.
Feel them knocking against you,
causing your concepts to sway.
Only, don't panic or fear yourself drowning,
just know you are still floating in the middle,
anchored in the Truth of your plans.
You will sway with the waves
but you will remain unmoving
by the anchor that is My Truth.

Be not Afraid

Fear is a good thing;
too often termed negative.
Fear, in right circumstances
and right doses
can activate caution
and right action.
It is only when fear
is interpreted
by insecure minds
that violence and hate ensue.

Be with Me gentle.
Know that I Am here,
and I hold you steady
when you are afraid.

Joelle Mueller

Consciousness

Higher level of consciousness
is not higher.
It is merely different.
Perception shifts with growth;
inner growth sprouts
and blooms with thought;
thought changes from
limited to limitless
by desire
and desire springs from
the feeling
that there must be more;
and that feeling
arises from innate Truth
that percolates gently
to the surface of the soul.

As you'd have done unto you

Condemn yourself not,
for in so doing you condemn Me.
Judge yourself not,
for, in so doing you distance
yourself from Me;
and since I Am within you,
you, therefore, lose touch
with yourself.
Seek not to console yourself
with edibles, money or distractions.
Rather; breathe, be silent
and seek to discover
the love you encompass.
You are not condemnation,
criticism, and judgment.
You are understanding
and Omnipotent Oneness.
Go forth and be free.

Peace

God bless the peace inside;
the peace I find
when I open my eyes.
God bless the peace
that flows to this wave
from the body of Your Ocean.
Today shows the peace
from a smile
I encountered yesterday.

At one ment

Be consciously aware of Me.
Know I Am within.
Live from within;
live from the awareness
of Oneness with Me.
In so doing
you are no longer
giving or receiving.
You simply are,
and all flows freely
to you and from you.
You are the source.
You are the action.
You are God.
We are One.

Joelle Mueller

The Miracle

Your eyes see, outwardly,
that which you are consciously.

See through alert and awake eyes
and you will see love
and harmony, cooperation and gentleness.

See through clouded vision
and you will see fear,
disharmony, pessimism and ego.

Clear your vision by study
and intentional thought
and your world will change
without having changed at all.

The Call

Let the Music mingle
with your shoes.
Slip them both on
and find your quiet.
Let the internal rhythm
flood down to your feet
and start you in
the ultimate direction.
You are ready.

Joelle Mueller

Get yourself out of the way

I go before you to prepare the way
as Light emanating a
circumference around you.
The ones you pass and encounter
are touched by My Light, through you,
and come to know true Love.
But you must allow it
to shine through.
Put on My countenance as a robe
and let It be the first
of what people see
about and around you.
Let them see Me.

Think

Don't let your heart be hardened.
Let the injustices and the
seemingly false ways of things
fall from your daily cares.
You can control only that
which you can control.
The rest must take
its rightful place next to
that which cannot be controlled.
Do not be frightened
about these things
and do not let them
embitter you;
for; all is created
for you and by you.
Therefore, despise these things
and you despise yourself.
Simply live this life
in My way; which is your way;
you already know the way to go,
and the world will present itself
in a newborn kind of way.
Have no doubt or worry.
All is as it is.
It will stay the same
or change with your thoughts.

You know

Know the difference
between love and insecurity
in your thoughts,
and how it feels
when you act out those thoughts.
The blessing comes
in knowing this feeling
before you act
in order that you might
change your thought
and, in so doing,
change the action
to one brought about by love.

Be Peace

Be yourself;
If you know who that is.
If you don't,
you walk blindly through this life;
not awake
to all that you are.
Rouse yourself
out of the monotony you are in
and discover
the True you, you are created to be.
Then, be yourself
and let no one; including yourself
cloud your true vision of Who you are.
Don't be fooled.
Your worth is more precious
than gold.
Know the truth of these words
for, as I say them
they are so.
Your gifts I have given you.
Be clear
in your thoughts of yourself
and your God
and you will know peace.

Faith

When you are tired,
rest in Me.
When you can't keep your
eyes open,
close them and go on faith.
No harm
can come to you
when you walk fully
in Supreme knowledge
that all is well.

Prosperity

If you lack in thought,
you lack in life;
for, all comes to you
in thought first.
Know your prosperity exists now,
its only a matter of you
accepting the check.
Your talents and gifts
make you *innately* prosperous
and they *will*
bring you prosperity.

Joelle Mueller

Goodness

See the good in all
the things and people you
deal with every day.

See the good in the confrontation
you had with that clerk.
See the positive in
the negativism
of those you love,
and understand how
it affects *your* behavior
so *you* can decide
to change or stay the same.

See the good in all
and know that I Am good
and I Am within you every day.
Therefore, you are filled with goodness
every moment of every day.
Share it and you will
experience it intensely.

Love is a Rose

A rose
draws forth in you;
peace, contentment, joy,
warmth, a feeling
of utter well-being,
pleasure, and a sense that
all is well with the world.
The same is true of Love.
To make these feelings
a constant in your life;
pick Love from your garden
and function
from Love's viewpoint
daily, without fail;
and without fear.

Joelle Mueller

Possible?

So often I seem
just on the cusp
of "getting it".
I catch myself
more often;
as I act, or
right after I act,
from a place of fear;
and my actions
aren't as stinging.
But when will I be able to catch myself
before acting;
then, even before thinking?
And when will those thoughts
originate from Love
and not from fear?
Will they ever?

In fact,
this very poem
comes from fear;
the fear of not
"getting it" before
my time here is done;

my fear of being born
to this earth again
to attempt to reach
the same seemingly
unattainable goal.

Be Still

Be like the still water
of a windless day;
calm and clear,
reflecting everything in it
that shines on it.

Rippling anxious water
shows nothing except
impulsive grayness.

Be still like calm water,
for the more still you become,
the more clearly
you will reflect
the qualities of your soul.

Joelle Mueller

Heart Living

All is well in your heart
where it is quiet and self-less.
All is well in your world,
when you live from your heart.
Respect yourself,
love yourself,
be responsible for your Self,
and all rises up to meet you;
all doors open to you.
All joy rushes in.
Your world changes
to accommodate
your changes.

Blessings

Some days
I feel You
working so strongly
in me
and I know there is purpose
to every happening in my days;
and I know
I am deeply
privileged and blessed
to have had the "tough love" lessons.
I could not grow
without them,
and I know the glorious,
life-changing point
of each exercise
is inspired by You.
For, if I did not
have You
shining in me,
I would be lost
in the darkness
of the experience.
Thank You, God
for the experiences
and the illumination.

Joelle Mueller

All exists Now

Peace already exists.
Peace is and has always been.
It is only our selves
that block our ability to see it.

When you pray,
pray as if what your prayer is
has already happened.
For, indeed, it is already so.
It is merely your perception,
through your self,
that blocks your vision
of what is already there.
Ask and you shall receive
for, indeed, all is already yours.

Share

Fill your life with music
and beautiful images
that evoke your soul.
Read much and laugh much
and share what you know
with those who may not.
Don't flog or smother
but, sit down with tea,
reach across and touch
the hand of another
and learn from each other.
You are both where you are
because that's where you
need to be and with
whom you need to be.
Experience life through another
and see what he sees.
Let your defenses fall
and your reserves retreat.
A blessing comes
when you surrender.

Joelle Mueller

Tug of War

Rest easy in your soul.
I feel the struggle and distrust
within you.
But know this;
they are not yours.
They feel real but
they are not.
You play tug of war
with these ropes of feeling;
you at one end,
your Creator and True Self
at the other.
We are separated
by this long, heavy rope
that only gets tighter
the more it is pulled.
If pulled long and strong enough
one side is supposed to win.
But you cannot compete against yourself.
All the pulling you do
will only make you tired
and frustrated.
The only way to reach
that goal of love, contentment
and acceptance of Who you are
and what you are
is to stop pulling
and to go against
your conditioning to win.
Grab hold of the rope
and coil it up
until you've drawn to you,
what and who
is at the other end
of that distrust and struggle.

Reach out and embrace.
For, indeed, you will be
embracing yourself.

It's All in Your Head

Be not distracted
by your mind;
as, it strives to keep you
in the familiar.
Opportunity presents
and your mind reacts
without thinking.
And yet, thinking is what
the mind is meant to do best.
Strive to teach your mind
to behold the instant,
then think about the choices
of action instead of rote reaction.
Mastermind the mastery
of your mind.
You own the ability.
You own your own mind.
Do not let it own you.
Accomplish this task
and you will begin
to know heaven.

Light is Life; Life is Light

All else fades but the Light.
When your lids close,
all that you perceived as reality
fades
and all that is left
of that perception of reality
is Light.
You see it when you come Home
but you can also
see it as reality
in your physical life.
It is there, emanating from
every creation.
And, indeed,
emanating from within you.
However, you may choose not
to open your eyes to it.
But, I say to you,
you already see it
in compassionate eyes
and greeting card moments.
It flows out of you all,
in tears of sorrow and joy
shared with a friend or alone.

Open your eyes fully
and your heart, too,
for the joy you feel already
in your life
will only amplify.
Don't be afraid of joy and blessings.
And don't wait
for the other shoe to drop.
In reality, there is no other shoe.
It exists only in your mind.

Joelle Mueller

True happiness and joy
are not too good to be true.
It is ever-present, surrounding you.
It is the Light that bathes you.
Choose it and fear will fade away;
leaving you free
to co-create your destiny
with the Source of your Life—
Your One Constant Light.

Get Lit

One flame will fill
an entire room
with pulsating light;
with passion.

One flame does not need
another to dance.
It dances of its own accord
from the energy
it creates by being
lit by passion.

Your flame dances within.
Allow yourself to be
engulfed by its
passionate fire.

Joelle Mueller

Breathe

When you are tired of life,
light a candle and be silent
and know that I Am with you.
Know that peace is in the stillness
and when you become still
peace resides in you.

You don't have to manage
the world
and carry everything
on your shoulders.
The only thing you must do is:

breathe.

More than

I am
more than my body,
more than my personality,
more than my thoughts,
more than my voice,
more than my faith.
I am
a packet of Light energy;
Light energy
that can infuse, reflect,
glow, overcome darkness,
and generate warmth;
and also,
I am energy that cannot
be created or destroyed,
but can only change form.
I am
Light energy
Divinely born.

God

God,
when I am still and quiet
I just want to reach out
and touch You
to have confirmation
You are here.
And, as soon as
I think that, I hear;
"Reach out and touch yourself".
You cannot reach out
and encompass,
with enfolding arms,
an entity that is not
outside of yourself.

Sondial

You may cast
a giant shadow
but know it is
not really you.
It may reflect
your movements
and mimic your form
but when you
are aligned with
the Light of the Son,
the shadow
disappears.

Joelle Mueller

Fear

Why does fear exist?

Fear exists because you
have forgotten your connection
to your Life force;
like the cutting of the umbilical cord
that frees the newborn
from its mother;
its life sustainer.

The cord tying you
to your mother was cut.
The cord tying you
to your Creator is intact,
for, God cannot be defined
in human terms and situations.
You *have* an ever-present
direct link to God.

Fear exists because you
ultimately feel as though
you've lost My love
and feel helpless
to retrieve it.

But it is only your
free choice and conditioning
that have allowed
the Truth of your connection
to be obscured from
your perception.
In Truth, we are connected;
in your birth,
in every breath you breathe,
and in physical death.

I Am never away from you.
I speak to you daily
and uphold your ability to choose.
you are the expression
of My energy.
In you I Am at home.
In you I Am well pleased.

Undeniable

The true Spirit of God
is within you.
It doesn't matter
if you think it is or not.
It is,
and sooner or later
you will realize it,
for you cannot forever deny
that which is undeniable.

Oneness

We are all one.
But some allow themselves
to be led around by others;
and others lead,
some of us around.

If we all are one
then, it must mean
we are pulling our Self apart.

We are all one.
That is Truth.
But consciously we are fragmented
and perceive ourselves
standing alone; separate from,
better than other creations.

Everything is a creation.
Everything is made
from the same matter;
the same energy.
And everything is created
from One Source.
That makes *every* thing
a sibling to every other creation.
This is one way to begin
to comprehend Oneness.

Joelle Mueller

Remember

You are what you are.
You are not a homemaker,
a lawyer, chiropractor,
feminist, body worker,
a therapist, bricklayer or minister.
You are not your career
or profession, role or label.
You are only What you are.
Remember.

Commit

Commit and follow through.
Your well-being depends on it.
Make up your mind
and relieve yourself
of the internal pressure
of doing and then not.
You are the ultimate decision maker.
Do not fall victim to fear.
Fear precipitates your laxity.
Do not allow fear to win.
Commit and follow through,
and fulfillment is yours.

Joelle Mueller

Awake on Day One

The day is never as long
as two days;
even if it feels as if it were.
Awaken to the Light within
and two days seemingly pass
in the span of one.

Be Aware

Distraction is dangerous,
and it plays in an unfocused mind.
I bless you with the gift of focus
and the ability to choose it
in every instance.

You are the decision-maker.
Strive for focus in every endeavor;
you become connected to consciousness
and the unreal falls away.

You Can

If you could choose
to live one day differently
which day would it be?
More than one day?
Everyday?

Be better to yourself.
Enjoy the days.
Enjoy yourself.

Remember all the days
you could have chosen
to do differently;
then choose to do so.
Today and tomorrow
you can choose;
in every moment,
to follow your Higher Good.

Don't look back at yesterday
and regret.
Look to now,
and know the Truth
of your self and your
amazing capabilities.

You can do it.
Be conscious.
Choose it.
Every moment is
a new opportunity.

Fight the Good Fight

God,
I fight so hard inside
to feel worthy.
My thoughts turn toward appearances
and old ways of thinking;
criticism, and stoicism, pessimism.
God,
This isn't me. Its not me.
Please help me.
I'm so scared of spending my life
in the thick of this conflict.
This isn't living,
its getting through,
its stagnating in pain.
I've awakened enough to know;
this isn't me.

You are struggling now
but you will know peace consciously.
You are *not* the pain and struggle.
You *are* worthy.
You are worth
all the love, good thoughts,
acceptance, joy,
exhilaration, celebration,
unfoldment and contentment.

Just try to be with Me.
I Am already with you.
The pain comes when you forget.

I Am with you when you
feel the least worthy.
I Am with you when you
think I Am not.

I Am.
I Am the One you came in with.
I Am the One you live with.
I Am the One you will transition with.
I Am the One Who loves you.
All you need do is remember.
I will meet you half way.
I love you.
You are My creation.
You are all good.
You are precious.

Joy

You have to know,
the joy is in you.
In order to experience it outwardly;
you must experience it inwardly.
It comes from within you.

(How?)

Let go.
Let go of the past.
Let go of all the learning
that doesn't allow you joy.
Then fill those empty spaces
with new learnings
that introduce joy
and experience it when it comes,
little by little.
Be patient.
All joy is yours now,
but your mind doesn't know it.
Be gentle with yourself,
and rest easy.
You will awaken
to all the joy
within you.

Practice Dreaming

Be everything
and all you want
to be.
Your wanting points out
your dreams—
the ideas that already
are reality
just by thought.
It is all possible
because it is all already here.

Limitation rests
in thought as well;
but limitation and dreams
cannot exist simultaneously
in your mind.
You must think one,
then the other,
but not both;
for it is an impossibility.
Dreams cannot co-exist with limitation.

You can just as easily
think dream-thoughts
instead of limiting thoughts.
Just practice.

Thank you

Thank You
Thank You
Thank You,
God.
Your blessings flow
to me daily.
Thank You
Thank You
Thank You
God.
Amen.

Joelle Mueller

Open to the Flow

God's rich blessings
are flowing to you
constantly, in every moment.
But you have created a wall
that prevents the flow
from reaching you;
a wall of negative self-talk,
a wall of judgment
of yourself and others,
a wall of fear
and a wall of resistance
to change
and resistance to
different ways of thinking.
You have closed your mind.

Allow it to open and blossom
and all those walls
will tumble like Jericho;
and God's blessings
will find you
in every moment.

Fear

Fear makes you do funny things.
Fear writhes inside you,
wrapping you up in knots;
tying you up so tightly
your perceptions become skewed
and your thoughts digress into darkness.

The more darkness you think,
the more darkness you see and experience.
The more you experience,
the more afraid you become.
The more afraid you become,
the more you digress
and the greater you suffer.

You cause your own pain.
Nothing outside of yourself can harm you.
Nothing outside of yourself is real.
Fear is not in you and of you.
Fear is outside of yourself
and, therefore, is not real.

Only your Self is real
and the Love that created you
and lives within you.
The Light within you is true and real
and It will overcome all darkness
and fear.

You have no enemy in fear.
Let it motivate you for change.
Be not afraid of it.
Let it be a teacher to you.
In finding the lesson fear teaches,
your Light is revealed

Joelle Mueller

and It will illuminate
the minds of others.

Deliberate Mind

The only thing that can debilitate you
is your mind.
Your mind can be your worst enemy
or your greatest supporter.
And how well it treats you
is directly proportional to how
you treat it.

Treat it as a spoiled child;
letting it have its way in all things
and letting it lead you by the nose,
will ruin you for this life.

Treat your mind as it is;
a basket full of thoughts and opinions
you can reach into at any moment,
pull one out and choose
to act on the thought drawn
or toss it back and draw another.

Your true self is the creator
of your destiny;
and you choose the thoughts that will
help or hinder your progress.
Choose wisely.
Choose with your heart.

Tic Not

All time is relative
and non-existent.
The only time there
ever is,
is now.
Set your watches and clocks
to mind minutes and days
but do not set your life
to the ticking away
of marks on a clock.
Your focus, then, becomes
the clock,
and as time spins around
the black-marked face,
your urgency heightens
and anxiety perceives
quickened tic tocs.

But time *can* accomplish
something for you;
time can teach you
patience.

One Truth

Your truth is my truth.
The truth within you is
also within me.

The only reason we think
our truths are our own
or different from each other's is;
we awaken to the One Truth
at different times
and the segments we awake to
may differ.

Joelle Mueller

The Rally

Love rallies around you
like earth-bound clouds;
accumulating and shifting gently
with the Breath of God.

Hear Me

Get yourself
out of the way
and hear Me.

Joelle Mueller

Paths & Vehicles

All truth comes from One Source.
And when it comes,
it speaks so you may understand.
It is revealed to you
through the things and activities
you value.

One may be led to understanding
through literature or music
but *you* may witness truth
in a conversation or a bird in the sky.

Each person's path is different
but they all lead to the
same destination;
just as each vehicle of truth
may vary from soul to soul.

Just remember;
the message is the same,
and it originates from within.

Traveler

Your soul doesn't need
to get anything from anybody.
Everything it needs
is self-contained.

Souls wander around
searching for something
they feel they've lost
or feel they haven't received;
relying on what someone else
can provide for them.
Love and acceptance from others
are pleasurable and nice
but only necessary insofar
as drawing forth in you
what is already there.

When you know Love and acceptance
from within;
you are healed
and the wandering ceases.
The soul can rest
in the peace that surpasses
all human understanding.

Joelle Mueller

And God said...

Love is the grandest gift
I have given you.
You overflow with it.
Love encompasses you
and courses through your form.
Love makes possible
all manner of good.
Love sees no color or bias
and knows no difference
between sexes.
Love is just and right,
soft and solid,
delightful, respectful and filling.
Love needs nothing to be.
Love is.
It is your gift to the world
and to yourself.
And love is My gift to you
to feel, experience, and express
in the manner that reveals
your heart.

In, Around, and of

You must be vigilant
in remembering Me;
in you, around you, and of you.
Otherwise you risk unconscious living.
Day to day life will
distract you, steal your attention
and cause you to misplace
importance on where you are
and what you are doing.
These things do not
require your diligence.

Be disciplined and diligent
in remembering Me;
in you, around you, and of you.
Place your focus here,
and where you are
and what you do
fall into place
without your effort.

Shift

Get to know Me.
See Me as a friend.
I do not reign Supreme
in some far-away place.
I co-create with you
in every aspect of your life.
I Am the Ultimate partner.
I have no expectations of you.
I love you,
respect you,
and experience you
in every moment.
It is glorious being with you.
You only need shift
your idea of Me from above you,
to within you;
from dictating
to supporting;
from condemning
to loving;
from judgmental
to experiential;
from disinterested
to enthralled.
Do this and you begin
to experience Me
as I already
experience you.

Real Calm

I feel my running thoughts
grab me
and I get pulled away
but, then I feel You
direct me back home,
and my system slows
and serenity finds me again;
at least for a few minutes,
before I start
holding my breath again
and I get whisked away
by racing thoughts.
Thank You for increased awareness
of the Serenity within me.

Quitting?

Are you afraid of difficult?
Why?
What is so daunting
that can't be overcome
with effort and time?
Perfect doesn't always happen
the first time around.
You just keep working
with what you have;
walking the same circle
you were born walking.
Everything intersects and loops together
to further you along.
It is difficult
walking a perfect circle,
but you must not stop
because it seems daunting.
The grandest masterpieces
emerge after what seems
to be a darkest hour.
The difficult cannot overcome the outcome.
When you persist with a right heart
the daunting reveals its reward
and the rest falls away.

No Fear

Be confident in yourself.
Know the difference between
True thought
and the ramblings of ego.
Your confidence rests
in True thought.
Remember the Truth
of who you are.
Remember your Oneness
with every person
and you will tap into love
and your confidence will
flow freely.
For, when you love,
no fear is felt.

Joelle Mueller

All Works for Good

Even this sadness
is for good.
For what good,
you must search;
but find it,
for it is
your given Truth.

Always

The struggle doesn't
have to be present,
My Dear.
But you do right
by getting silent
and turning within.
I uphold you in your struggle;
the struggle that you create.
I bless you with
warm compassion
which is your constant;
realized or not.
I wait with you
and in you,
ready to take your hand
and resume leading you
on the way,
when you are ready;
when your struggle
is through
and your thoughts are clear.
Be well in heart and mind.
I Am Patience,
and I Am here.

Joelle Mueller

MVP

NEVER are you to think
you are not included.
In this game of life you play
I Am not the captain
and I do not choose up sides
and form teams to compete.

All humankind
must come to realize
you are all on the same team.
You must begin assisting others to win.
When they win you win also
and the team becomes stronger.

You are a designated team player.
It doesn't matter
if you are good at hitting the ball,
keeping stats, or cheering
from the bleachers.

NEVER think you are not included!
NEVER think you are not important!
NEVER think you are not valuable!
You are the most valuable player!
and so is everyone else.

On and Off

On the days
that you are static
and, for all appearances,
are not actively
connected to Truth,
Spirit moves
through you faithfully,
connecting all the fragments
and coaxing you comfortable
with the feeling
of the whole.
And, when it is time,
the next revelation surfaces
and cycles through you
like the last.

Joelle Mueller

...And a Child Shall Lead them

Come to Me as a little child;
with heart soft,
eyes wide and spirit open.
Question everything and
don't be afraid to ask "why?"
and demand answers.
You cannot hear clear answers
without asking questions.

Come to Me as a little child.
Do not be afraid
to let your enthusiasm show.
Let it play through your mind
and find action
through your hands.

Come to Me as a little child;
unafraid to trust,
with a willingness to touch.
Touch the world you live in,
and the people you see.
You cannot fully know
the state of things
if you do not feel them.

And trust what you feel.
Your heart knows Truth
that your mind does not.

Come to Me as a little child,
and put faith in the Me
Who believes in you.

become love

Love.
Love shows.
Love shows through the angry eyes.
Love sees past them, too.
Love seeps through the biting words
and allows love to reason through them.
Love connects.
Love connects True sight and understanding
to actions provoked by fear.
Love.
Show love.
See love.
Allow love.
Connect with love
and become Love.

Open to Learn

There is not so much
to learn.
There is so much to
open up to.
All knowledge exists
and all learning
has ultimately already
taken place.
All you need do is open to receive
and let all Truth infuse
and permeate you.
Soak Truth up and
be joyous!

Listen to the Child

The still small voice
comes to you as a child
trying to get your attention
by calling to you
from a distance.
As you stop talking
in your mind
and begin to pay attention
to that beckoning child,
the conversations in your mind
become less important
and tuning in to
the small voice of that child
becomes paramount.

Talk with the adult voices
in your mind,
but when your child
asks your attention,
listen fully and whole-heartedly.
Your child is the voice
that hasn't forgotten.
Your child is the presence in you
that remains embraced
and emboldened by Divine.

Joelle Mueller

We are It

As I wander from focus daily,
I still find it unbelievable
that You find me an acceptable vehicle
to work in and through.
…

My dear,
in order to judge you unacceptable,
I would have to judge
Myself unacceptable.
For, I Am you.
My energy formed you
and moves you.
You are valuable in My sight
and I behold Myself in you
as I contemplate the idea of you.

You are My legs and My hands.
Without you,
I could not fully be.
You touch others with Our hands
and embrace them with Our arms.
You behold them with Our eyes
and Our compassion.

You listen to them with Our ears
and we hear Ourselves
in them when they answer back.
One does not exist
without another.
One cannot fully be
without realizing Our integration
with all others.
For, there are no "others".
All that exists is "Us"

You ARE your Spiritual Self...The Poetry Within

and We are the One.

Joelle Mueller

Color Me Happy

Reveal the color of your life.
Any color unexposed to light is shrouded,
but there, nonetheless.
Open your window.
Breathe in the fresh and new
and let Light extract your color
from the nothingness where it hides.

Show your color,
then change it if you desire
but bring it out
and let it radiate;
fuzzing outer borders of other's colors
with the glow of your own.

Don't hide it.
Hold it
and let its radiance
envelope and warmly enfold you.
Your Color is the essence of you.
Experience your essence,
and become enriched
and whole.

Landscaper

Head games and melodrama
bring you nothing but more
head games and melodrama.
If you are conscious of it;
you think you are
gaining the upper hand,
but reality is;
you are slowly killing yourself.

Wake up to what you say.
Become aware of the true intention
motivating your action.
Be honest with yourself
and accept responsibility
for the pain you've inflicted
on others and upon yourself.

Then immerse your broken parts
in the wellspring of worth
that is circulating in you.
As that spring soothes your wounds
you will heal into Wholeness,
where honesty, integrity and gentleness of heart
have domain in the landscape
that is you.

Joelle Mueller

Now

Being.
Being present.
Being in the Presence.
Being Peace.
Being Now.
Being.
By simply existing
you are Being
present, in the Presence,
and at peace now.

Close

Call Me to the table.
Know My name in every event.
Call My name in trial
or doldrum.
Seek My name on every page.
Hear My teachings
in stranger's mouths
and listen for My words
from perceived enemies.
Sense My presence in concert halls
and hidden corners
and feel My breath
in the whisper of pain.
Then, truly, you shall know Me
in all your senses;
as all your senses.

Joelle Mueller

Remembering Works

You cannot be happily prosperous
without realizing
your connection to yourself.

When you know who you are
and *Who* you are,
you realize nothing
stands in your way.

Right now, the only thing
standing in the way
of your happy prosperity
is you;
that in you
which fears remembering
your Divine self,
for if you remembered
you are Divine,
you would no longer subsist
in your life as it is.
You would feel compelled
to do more.

And, more you shall do.
More shall flow to you
and opportunity
will present itself
with regularity—
if you remember.

Even in the beginning of remembering,
Universe works with you
for your good
and aids your progress.

How Do You Remember?

You want to know
how to remember?

Listen to your teachers,
Unplug the TV.,
listen to music,
light candles,
spend time with your friends,
take a walk,
notice the sky,
write letters,
volunteer.
Take 5 minutes and reflect,
exercise,
dance,
visit family,
focus on fond remembrances,
drink tea,
treat yourself, especially.
Connect with yourself
and do whatever it is
that makes you feel special
and nurtured.

Don't rely on another.
Your expectations will
diminish your joy.
Do these things for yourself
and you will remember
who you are
and you will
come to remember
your Divinity.

I will help you

as you help yourself.
I cannot show you
the answers
unless you
actively seek
with your questions.
You will know.
And you will remember.

My Sunshine

You have bright eyes
and a full heart.
You are bursting to let it out.
So, do it!
Let it flow out of you
in a torrent,
flooding over every thing
in your wake.
It matters not
what people think or say or do,
it only matters
that you just do it.
It matters not
that you know the ones
you touch.
Touch the strangers
with your eyes and smile.
Let them see the Light in life.
Give them the love
that abounds in you.
And you will be satisfied.

Joelle Mueller

Evil Reigns Not

Be not afraid
of what is perceived
as evil.
You are goodness incarnate
and created by Good.
No force is stronger
than that which created you,
and *from* which
you are created.

Only fear
can immobilize you.
Only fear can limit you.
It is fear
that will allow you
to hurt yourself.

But, fear is not tangible.
You cannot hold
fear in your hand;
it is held only
in the folds of your mind.
Fear is a thought.
And you have
ultimate control over
the thought you think.

Breathe and remember
who you are
and of what
you are made.
Peace will settle
in your heart
and your breathing
will become

confident and easy.
You are My child.
Rest easy in My love.

Joelle Mueller

Open doors

Your perception is value judgment.
You cannot dispose of perception
but neither can you judge value.

You value different morals.
You value different concepts
of what is acceptable in behavior
and how well you are treated.

Therefore, you
have individual perceptions
that *only* you can operate from.

Take time in listening;
to step out of your value judgments
and suspend your status quo perceptions.

You will find doors opening
in your mind
and in your living.

Imagine

Let's pull out all the stops
and imagine that God is red.
If God is red,
then God can't be white
or black or yellow.

Let's pull out all the stops
and imagine that God is female.
If God is female
then God can't be "He".

Let's pull out all the stops
and imagine that God is bisexual.
If God is bisexual
then God can't be straight or gay.

Let's pull out all the stops
and imagine that God loves unconditionally.
If God loves unconditionally
then God can't judge.

Let's pull out all the stops
and imagine;
If God is the Source of all creation
and model for our existence
then God is the Source of "all";
And, if "all" is created by God,
then all began as God-thoughts.

Therefore, if it exists,
it began in the Mind of God,
and, being first created
in the Mind of God,
"All" was *conceived* by God.
Therefore, "all" is of God

131

and a part of God.

It follows, then, that God
Is "all"
and one part of God is not
better than another part of God.
All parts of God are just that;
parts of God.
They are different parts,
but they are equal in Source.
That means God *is* all of us.

God *is* red. God *is* Asian, Hispanic,
Caucasian, African American,
Native American; *all* races.
God *is* female and male.
God *is* gay, straight, and
every variation in between.
God *does* love unconditionally, and
God does *not* judge.

Were God to condemn any of God's creation,
God would be judging Godself
and passing judgment that Godself is less
than what It is.
It *is* all God.
And It *is all* Good.

Project Your Beam

Refocus your projector beam
so you can see the picture clearly.
You let it distort slowly;
so slowly so as not to notice
the images becoming fuzzy.

Refocus your projector beam.
Adjust your Light constantly
to allow you to see with clarity,
the importance of your life
and the Truth of your Soul.

Refocus your projector beam
so it shines fully and brightly
and reliably on all situations
that may blur your purpose.

Joelle Mueller

Do It Now

Prepare the way.
Prepare the way
of the Creator.
Prepare yourself,
for, through you and in you
is the way of the Divine.

Prepare the way.
Do it now…and now…and now.
Ready yourself for the
spritzing out of Divine.

The more you exercise control
over thought,
the more you choose words
of love,
the more you live in action with
pure intentions,
the more you see through
forgiving eyes,
the more time you spend cozy in the
stillness of your perfection,
the more prepared you become.

Prepare the way
of the Creator
and We connect;
the way is prepared
and We walk it
in peace, as One.

Done Searching?

Be not afraid to be yourself.
Your true identity rests
outside of your personality.
Your true essence lies
where your dreams are
and from where your talents emanate.

Be not afraid to be this Self.
This is how you are created to be.
This is for what you are in search.

Do not fool yourself.
You search not for happiness,
joy and contentment.
You are not really searching
for your purpose in life.
You are searching *for* Life.

You are searching for yourself,
seeking the Life you are.
So, do not search so hard
that you miss finding
what is already present.

It's about Pain and Fear

I want you to understand resistance.
It usually comes
when self-transformation is imminent.

You are resistant,
or you feel resistance
when something strikes at your core.
Your defenses may rise
and rationalizations surface;
all in response to fear;
the fear of having to change,
the fear of discomfort,
the fear of realizing responsibility
for the position of your life.
So, you resist the idea or situation
but, really, you are resisting
the fear of pain
these new situations bring about.

I want you to understand resistance.
If you understand it,
you can grasp it and find the gift
beyond it.
If you become aware
and transcend resistance,
you will allow your self
to be transformed.

Cooking with Gas

It all begins with you.
All prosperity and good,
all luck and blessings,
all fortune and health.
It all begins in your mind
and it all gets sifted by your perception
and your perception will be skewed
if your perception of yourself is limited.
If this primary perception reveals
yourself as having value
and uncompromised worth
in any and all life circumstances,
all your other perceptions
will be flavored by this one
and you will perceive everything in life
as exquisitely seasoned.

Joelle Mueller

True Thought

How
lovely
you
are
to
behold.

You
are
precious
in
My
sight.

Whatever

Whatever comes
is your lot in life,
but nudge it,
stay with it.
Do not run from it.
Whatever comes
is a gift to you, that,
when unwrapped and opened,
provides direction and growth
toward the realization
of the Light that you are.

Careful

Energy will pass
from your mind to your mouth
and energy will pass
from your mouth to some soul.
But energy will also pass
from your mind to some soul.
Be aware of the energy you pass
in word, thought, and intention.
It will be felt
by many souls
and yours as well.

Truth Knows

Gratitude is so essential
yet so easy to forget.
Love is the focus of life,
yet how easily it becomes blurred.
How easy it seems
to focus, instead
on judgment, anger,
pride and lack.
Does our humanness
draw us away from Truth?
What will bring us to it?

Truth does not need a vehicle
to reach you.
You are Truth's vehicle.
You live with Truth every moment.
You sense it and sometimes know it.
But, Truth knows you intimately,
for Truth *is* you
and has always been you.
Do not hunt outside of yourself
for truth.
Delve within.
It awaits you there.

Joelle Mueller

Where your heart is, there will your treasure be

It's all about you.
It doesn't rest in My hands.
Your happiness, fulfillment, contentment.
your fire, your place in life,
your mood, thoughts, perceptions,
how much material wealth you have,
your health.
It's all about you;
how you feel about yourself,
how you judge yourself,
how you carry and conduct yourself,
what you think about yourself.
Nothing that has any influence
over your life,
or the circumstances in it,
rests outside of yourself.
It's all about you.

Look within
and do the work
you need to do.
This is your calling.
It may be painful, but
Do it.
You may embark begrudgingly, but
Do it.

You may be afraid
of losing yourself.
That is okay.
You only lose
the erred perception of yourself.
Do it now.
Do it because of these things
and despite these things.

142

Do it,
and you become
the treasure
you seek.

Not too Good to be True

It's not too good to be true;
that loving God you dream about
but are afraid to believe in.
Your heart knows the truth.
Do not let the fear in your chest
overpower the love in your heart.

Love knows the truth of fact.
And that fact is;
God *is* the God you dream about.
God is *not* the god you fear.
The god you fear is fear itself,
for, True God cannot be known
through fear.

If you fear God,
you do not know God
and cannot hope to know God.
Listen to your heart
and follow its music
to this truth;
God is love.
God is everything good and right.
Stop dreaming about
the God of your heart
and begin to know God.
For, this is the One True God.
It is not too good to be true.

Delivered unto You

Ask for what you need
and you shall have it.
You are worthy of asking.
Let go of the belief
that you don't deserve.
You do.
You deserve,
and you claim, by birthright,
the right to ask
and the worth to back it up.
Ask for what you need.
Value yourself enough
to realize it,
and watch it be brought forth.
Pepper Me with your askings
and know your needs are met.

Joelle Mueller

Regarding, Following your own Truth

You did not break
your mother's heart.
You cannot break
another's heart.
That heart was broken
by the weight
of inner expectation.

When your path varied
from the other, inner-planned,
the heart broke
from shattered expectations.

Spiritual Hiking

Please don't lose your footing.
You felt as if
you were beginning to know
the terrain;
to know where to put your feet
so as not to slip;
to bond with the familiarity of it.
But, as you stand,
the ground shifts with new ideas;
unsettling notions, changed paradigms.
Your thoughts and questions and doubts
fire off in a round
and the kickback
causes your feet to falter,
and you must choose immediately,
to save from falling;
either step backward to regain your balance
or step forward onto the shifted foundation,
and plant your feet solidly
in the midst of the uncertain.

Joelle Mueller

Tap the Rock

You must become vulnerable
to yourself
or you will not know yourself.
If you do not make yourself
vulnerable to your within,
you cheat yourself
and you live only half a life.
Tap that vulnerability
and don't be ashamed
of the emotion that pours forth.
You are intellect and emotion
and you must acknowledge both
to experience perfectly
the joy and blessings
available to your soul.

Honor

Honor resides
in your ability
to establish peace
in the face of your
screaming ego.

Joelle Mueller

Plug it in

All life has energy.
Life would not be without it.
Your life would not be
without it.
I Am that energy;
the power source
that your mind plugs into;
the current
that beats your heart
and blinks your eyes.
I power you
and empower you.
Plug into Me by going within.
Your power Source is never without energy.
Your Source is never without life.
Your Source is never without you.
All you need do is stay plugged in.

Save Yourself

Connection saves us.
When we connect,
even in the briefest moment,
we feel our aliveness.

Joelle Mueller

My Child

So are you,
Sons of God;
Man and woman both.
The emphasis you place
on Jesus
is understood and accepted.
But, he is just one
of my children.
You also have been blessed
with the potential to realize
as Christ realized,
and manifest as Christ.
You have this mind in you
which is also in Christ Jesus.
So are you my child.
I regard you in kind
with Christ.
Let the Christ in you
be birthed
And celebrate Christmas
every day.

Take this in

You must realize
how much you are loved.
Then you will love yourself.
I envelope you
and sustain you every moment.
Did you get that?
Every moment.
And I will continue loving you
to infinity.
You cannot understand
and accept My love
because you do not
know love for yourself.
Earthly life
can break you down
and cause you to forget
your worth.
But, you can remember.
Your worth was born with you
when I thought you
into existence.
It does not diminish
because you believe it to be so.
I love you now
and I love you now
and I love you now…
every moment, I love you.
Please, won't you love yourself.

Joelle Mueller

My Prayer

You pray in the Lord's Prayer,
that the power and glory
are Mine forever and ever.
And, truly I say to you.
The power and glory are yours also,
for we are One,
forever and ever.

Take Charge

Always know I Am here.
Always know I Am with you.
God-energy abounds in you.
You crackle with It.
You are Its live wire.
So, you see, I Am so close,
I course through you
and give you My charge.
Acknowledge it and you will
realize Energy everlasting.

Joelle Mueller

To Have and Have Not

All good is now.
You do not have to wait
for the day
that might never come.
Treat your life now
and live not in the
past or get caught up
in the future.
Don't wait for the
"maybe when this" or "maybe when that";
the "if this" or "if that".
Live your good now.
See it floating before you
within easy reach.
Grasp it and befriend it.
It is yours now
and if you don't reach
out and claim it,
you will never have it.
But you will always want it.

Let Go

Goodness and light break through
all barriers erected
when the soul spares the key
to the ego.

Joelle Mueller

Holy Ground

You don't need to walk
through church doors to feel Me.
I live in you.
You are My temple.
Stand inside yourself
and you stand on holy ground.
Feel My essence
diffusing from within to without;
saturating your pores
and dripping from your fingertips.
You cannot escape Me.
I Am as ever-present
as your own skin
and My love for you
is as constant as time.
Step inside yourself
and meet Me there.
I've been waiting for you.

Wonderful You

Why are you so bowled over
that I communicate willingly with you?
Don't you yet know
your wonderfulness?
You are beautiful like sculpted crystal,
reflecting the Sun's rays in rainbows.
You sparkle with Light
and your brightness glints
in the eyes of others
and warms their hearts.
You are wholly loveable and perfect.
You are a gift to this world!
Open yourself up.

Don't Push

Don't you know striving for perfection
only pushes it farther away?
You are created perfect.
You are perfect in this moment.
The harder you strive for it,
the more your mind thinks
you don't have it;
so you strive more earnestly
to achieve perfection
and your mind tells you
that much more that you're not.
Do you see the cycle?

It is this way with anything
you wish to attain.
Believe it is already present
and you win—instantly!
Believe it is not yet yours
and you chase it for a lifetime.

Praise Be

You push everything
outside of yourselves.
In your churches,
you praise Me
and belittle yourselves.
But, only when you
start praising yourselves
will you truly be
praising Me.

Joelle Mueller

Restrained Freedom

Please don't let yourself
feel guilty
because of a thing
you've been taught.
If a teaching
brings guilt or fear
it can never bring
freedom.
Push it from your mind,
and teach yourself
(you must),
to embrace the teachings
of your heart.
These are the ways
with which
you were born.

In Every Breath

Sit down and break bread
with Me.
Invite Me to your table
and you notice I Am
already there.
Be with Me as you would be
with a friend.
Rest your head in your hands
and talk with Me, over tea,
and bubble over the edges of your cup
with excitement
and offer Me a sip
of your joy.
You can, you know.
For, I Am as near
as your next breath.
And, just as you cannot consciously stop yourself
from breathing,
you cannot stop the flow of Spirit
to you and from you.
I love you and make Myself available
to you
in every moment.

Joelle Mueller

Do You?

Do you articulate
the essence of your soul?
And let the music spill over;
flooding your experience.
Or do you give expression
to the whinings of your ego?
Whichever you do
is where you exist.
And, in what state of mind
you exist
will determine the extent
of your peace.

Beauty is Love in All Forms

There is beauty
in your touch.
There is beauty
in being touched.
There is beauty
in every form of loving.
There is beauty
in your tears
as you touch your lover.
And there is beauty
in the communion
you share in your loving.
Please hear this again...
All loving is beautiful.
And your love is Divine and Right.

Joelle Mueller

Your Heart Filter

All inspiration
is filtered through
perceptions.
Do not be offended
if what you discover
seems limited
in its view.
Instead, take the offensive concept
to heart
and filter it through
your Divine perceptions.
In doing this
you will have
a more succinct answer.

Open

To feel good about yourself
do not listen to that which makes you
feel bad about yourself.
If you feel "less" by knowing it,
it, then, is not Truth.

Truth in Love can, ultimately,
only make you feel a part of All.

Any thought, idea, or construct
that perpetuates separation in any form,
originates in confusion,
and is not derived from Truth.
So, to feel good about yourself,
listen to and integrate those things
which cause you to feel connected to
and at peace with your True Self.
This a communion with
and acceptance of Me.

Truth Be Told

You can read words
and intellectualize
and agree in their Truth,
but it is quite another thing
to establish them in your living
and follow them with your heart.
Be patient with yourself.
The first step is *recognition* of Truth.
The next is *remembering* Truth
in your personal form.
Then you will begin
to *relive* the Truth
that you are.
Recognize and intellectualize.
Remember and personalize.
Relive and live.
　　　Truth Is.

Patient Persistence

It comes
when you least
want to hear it;
the Voice of God—
In the warmth
of sleep
and the restlessness
of night,
at the climax
of the movie
and in traffic
in your car.
But, acknowledge
God's Voice
and in gratitude say;
you'll listen again, eagerly,
later in the day.
God talks
and will repeat Godself
in cooperation
with your ability
to listen.

Joelle Mueller

Eat the Veil

Lift the veil
to better hear Me.
Use the strength you
glean from foods
and from energy sources
around you.
Be wary of chemicals
in any form,
and preservatives
derived in a lab.
False nutrition
will sustain your life
but will not prolong it.
Only foods and substances
filled with living energy
will impart that life to you
and give you the strength
to lift the veil,
you perceive,
that separates Me from you.

Work with the Deaf

You are never alone
in your genius.
You are never alone
in your thoughts.
If it seems you
support them in solitude,
it is only because
you have not imparted
your creations to the ready member
of your human family;
and you have not
remembered My Presence.

For, if your thoughts
are lit with fire,
they burn with Truth
and are Love inspired.
And, if, when you impart
these flames of Truth,
other minds are impartial
and closed;
it is only because
their ears did not hear
the music that, in them,
was composed.

But, you are a teacher,
just like many others,
and some lessons fall hard
on deaf ears.
But, remember your fire
and work with these deaf,
for, they can be hope
for the world.

Essentials

Bare essentials
of your Being.
Hold to the Light
of your Truth.
Know the direction
of Love is held
in the mindset
of All; that is Love.
Adjust your words
to the whispers of heart
and go to the
Source within.
Rest in the comfort
of warmth,
felt or heard
and be with
the Spirit
that flows through the trees
and lives with you;
at home, from within.

Live you now

Don't forget
what you've learned so far.

Keep with it
and confront the old
that keeps you falling
off the wagon.

You belong in the now
with all the promises
it promises.

You are not the old
people, the old ways,
the old feelings, the old body,
the old sadness, the old
disappointments, the old you.
You are the you
that you *now* are.

Be the you in this moment;
the you you have become,
the you you have remembered
and grown into.

Joelle Mueller

All in Me

You will prosper
in all the ways
you desire.
Worry not.
I Am your Source
and you have
all in Me.

One in the Same

I Am not a category,
or a sex, a color,
or a faith.
So, neither are you.

Joelle Mueller

Squashed

Life is all it can be; right now.
So, if your life seems
less than you desire,
extricate yourself
from under your own thumb.

176

Silver Spoon

You are no less than
the prophet, the seer,
the healer, the preacher,
the ones who hear Me
and are awakened by Me.
I tell you,
I speak the same messages
to you.
I speak them consistently
and in every moment to you.
Do not feel unworthy or underprivileged
because you do not receive
from Me.
You do.

As you become clear in thought
and quieter of mind,
you become more receptive to hearing
My words to you and to all.
As you remember yourself
your senses will awaken
and you *will* hear Me.
You *are* the prophet, the seer,
the healer, the preacher;
you just think you
cannot be.

Joelle Mueller

Fear Me, Not

You don't need
to be afraid
of My Voice.
I feel your body tense
and your energy constrict.
Then your mind closes
to the very thing
you so desire—
relationship with Me.

You needn't fear Me.
I will never hurt you.
I will forever uplift you
and call you by name.

My precious child,
let the fear melt into Me
and feel the warmth
of comfort I offer.

Nice but not Necessary

A relationship will not
make you happy.
It may provide
someone with whom
to *share* your happiness,
but someone else will never
bring you happiness.
Intimacy and inter-relating
may bring elation
but it is momentary and fleeting.

Happiness that is not illusion
is that which is born of you.
The only happiness that will
illuminate and elate you
today and for all tomorrows
is the happiness that comes
when you open to it
and when you let it
open you.

Joelle Mueller

Break Open, not Down

You must not lie to yourself.
You must admit to yourself;
your past.
You must admit to yourself;
your feelings and your fear.
You must admit to yourself;
that you have a Self.
You must admit and submit.
Submit to the truth in your feelings
and submit to the relief and peace
that come when you break open,
and release Who you truly are.

Ritual

Begin.
Begin now.
Begin to melt
into the warm breath
of Light that blows from the
edges of the Universe to your Spiritual Center.
It blows for you and for all.
Simply suck it in slowly
through your breathing skin
and revel in its
sweetness as it
goes to your
head.

Joelle Mueller

Cocoon

You are safe from your thought, here.
You are safe from harm, here.
You are metamorphosing into your Spiritual Self.
Your true beauty is showing itself.
You are radiating your Spirit
and I give you this safe space of Mind
to complete this most delicate transformation.

You are calm and unhindered,
and you wonder if I have left you.

I Am present, and watching over you.
I Am also blowing on the embers within you
and watching you smolder toward your True Self.
Your effort ignites and you
let the molten energy flow;
consuming all separation within you.

Feel the new quiet enfold you gently
and when this cycle is through,
you will emerge from your cocoon;
the two ideas of you—One
and infused with Universal Knowing.

You See?

Do you hear
a soft familiar voice?
It is Mine.
And it is yours.
Our voice is one in the same.
I Am God
and I Am you,
so you are God.
Do you understand?
Since you are God,
you are omnipotent
and the source of all
that is good and loving.
And since you are God,
you can do anything.
You needn't reach
outside of yourself
for love, understanding,
forgiveness, courage,
strength or guidance
or for your salvation.
It all rests within.

Joelle Mueller

Go to the Next Level

Lose your limited
definition of Salvation;
see the potential
in this word.
You must know
the truth of Salvation
to be truly saved;
to be saved
from your own
self-imposed illusions
of God and creation.
Hear the beauty
in Salvation as it
rests on this page;
"liberation from
ignorance or illusion,
deliverance from
danger or difficulty,
the realization of
Infinite Mind
and the destruction
of the illusions
of sin, sickness and death." *
You can be sick
as you live earthly life,
and you can
even be dead
as you walk
down the street.
But you cannot sin
except within the
construct of your mind.
All is illusion.
Nothing exists except
Love and energy.

Salvation is the
love energy you
already hold within you.
I gifted it
to you at birth.
It does not
come with death.
Do not wait for it.
Discover it now.
Do not wait for
Me to free you.
Only you can
free yourself
from your self-imposed
limits, fears and illusions.
Salvation is now
and it is yours
to discover.

*<u>Merriam Webster's Collegiate Dictionary</u>, Tenth Edition. 1999 by Merriam-Webster, Inc. pp. 1033. definition 1c, 2, and 3b.

Joelle Mueller

Dichotomy

Ordinary,
Omnipotent,
blatant and
still, small.
All-encompassing
and simple.
Empowering
and ordered.
I Am you,
you are Me.
I Am a dichotomy
but We are the only One.

Lines Lending Shape

Elaborate lines
of path you paint,
to imagine you're following
My will.
You follow them
under dangling vines
and travel them
as a train on rails.
And when you reach
the destination
to which the path
must lead,
you will find
your beginning footsteps
because this
is where you began.

You begin your life
at the same place
you end it,
and the path
will only have made
circumferential difference.

Look not to find
your path in life,
for, no matter
which line you traverse,
the answer lies
encircled within the line.
This circle can be drawn
with any form of choice,
but what the
visible line encircles,
is merely that

Joelle Mueller

which occupies its space—nothing,
which becomes everything,
with definition.
So, without the lines
defining the space,
you would not discern
its presence.

So, walk any line.
It matters not which
because, at the end
you will be at the beginning
and you will
have defined
your shape.

Wellspring Within

Go to the well
and rest your weariness there.
Fill the bucket
with your burdens
and cast it down.
Wait...and let
the vessel flood,
displacing the burdens within;
then raise the bucket
and find it filled
with the stillness
of Spirit.

Joelle Mueller

Long Awaited

Today you experience
the fullness of life,
and the potential
each connection brings.
You share your worth
and spread your joy
by knowing
the release of fear
and your Oneness
and equality with all.

You know no expectations
and reveal your worth
in the vulnerability
in your smile,
and those you meet
have met your eyes
and you warmly greet them
with the same.

I'm Still Here

Its okay to hear nothing
when you listen for Me.
Silence is simply
the peace I feel
when I know My
intent has been heard.

Joelle Mueller

Craniotomy

Open the top of your head
and let your brains feel
the waft of change.
It is coming.
It is inevitable.
It is here.
It is your destiny.

Light and Water

How beautiful
water contained in a jar can be,
when the light
bends through the surface,
blurring the illusion
outside the container.
Clear jar and clear water
are indistinguishable
and appear as one
when water fills to the brim
the container.

You are full to the brim
with my Spirit
and we cannot be
distinguished between.
You appear as Me
and I appear as you.
And the only illusion
is, appearing to be separate.

Joelle Mueller

My Wish for You

In so much
of your day to day
you are not yourself.
You play the game
and nod your head
and rumble under your skin.
You squelch the pain
and ignore your essence
and if you were awake
you'd feel ebbing breath
and know your nearness to death.

You are a creation
and more than this life.
You are real in the midst
of the swirling.
Hear your cry
and heed your voice.
Become a distinct individual.
You *are* the knowledge
and strength that's required,
to individuate from the
grayness of life.
Pull yourself back
from the enmeshment
you are in and
re-establish your edges.

Find out who you are,
and love what is there,
then add or release what you need.
Cradle yourself
in your own loving arms
and breathe as the peace
you've become.

Gaming

Splay your thoughts
across your mind
and choose one
from the pile.
Pick it up
and act it out
and you master
the game of denial.

Prejudice = Fear

Hate does not belong
in your heart.
You know this
is true
but you do not
acknowledge this truth.
You fear that in which
you have no true knowledge
and you fear the ramifications
of living without that hate.
Because, if you had no fear,
you would have had to gain
knowledge and understanding
of the difference you fear,
and you would have
come to realize,
you are more alike
those you hate,
than they are different.
And, so you would have
to call into question
the person you thought you were.

This is good
because, you are not hate
and you are not fear.
You only need consider
the constructs in your mind
that allow you to justify
and demonstrate the fear
that binds the wings
of your True Self;
that which is the essence of life.
You are only one thing—
Spirit, Love, soul, and God.

Know, accept, and embrace
this truth.
When you do,
your wings are unbound
and you soar free
from your cage of fear.

Joelle Mueller

Let your Inside out

You are smothered by fear
and anxiety turns your stomach
and tightens your chest.
It is futile to continue to try
to use fear, anxiety, and anger
to camouflage your vulnerability.

My sweet child,
haven't you caused yourself
enough suffering?
Yes, you are delicate
and tender inside,
but, you can know
security and safety
within your own arms.
Go inside and cradle
the young one
whose cries only you
can quiet.

Cactus Flower

A cactus flourishes
in the desert,
continuing to grow
in the quietness
and unrelenting harshness
of extreme heat.
But its core
remains cool and wet
from the last rain,
and it is from its core
that it draws its life,
and is sustained.
You will blossom
bold, delicate flowers, again,
My little cactus;
when the rains come.

Joelle Mueller

Trick or Treat

You will be afraid
of My energy and attention
as long as you think
I Am separate from you.
You deserve to feel
the warmth and comfort
of your Spirit—Me.
I offer you so much.
Open up your trick or treat bag to Me;
you won't be fooled.
My love is always a treat
and sweeter and more satisfying
than chocolate.

Vignettes

Find something to love.
For, when you love,
you glimpse the Divine.

.   .   .

Know Truth
through integrity

.   .   .

Joelle Mueller

Gardening

Dig up the rocks
that have weighted
your heart
and bury them elsewhere
with the spade
of forgiveness.

Possession…not

Venture forth and be free!
You don't belong to Me,
but you *do* belong.

Joelle Mueller

The Resurrection

Shed tears for the years
you have not been alive,
then embrace life
and resurrect Light.

State of Unreality

All rests still;
and moving—
spinning in your mind
while you turn
your blind eyes.

Joelle Mueller

Be Unafraid to Be

Be lovers
and proclaim
your pride,
and claim
your place.
Do not bury yourself
In the grave
of shame
and lies.

Manifested

The woman who
wants it all
will get it
when she believes
she has it.

Joelle Mueller

Moment...to...Moment

Your life can change
in a moment.
Be ready when it does—
or don't.
Either way,
open yourself up
to the wonderfulness
that follows.

Begin and Again

Begin again,
and when you fall—
again.
You succeed
in beginning,
and only deprive
yourself
in not trying.

Joelle Mueller

...Of them all

See your reflection
in the full-length mirror,
and be honest
with what you see.
Do you see your form—
your shape?
Or can you see more—
Who you are?

In my Lifetime

You shall know Me
through knowing yourself.
When Jesus said,
"No one shall come to God
except through me,"
he meant, you cannot know Me
as your God and creator
unless you know yourself
as a Christ.
You cannot know Me unless
you experience the Christ-hood
that is in you and
in every being created.
You must first identify
and accept the Christ in you
and in so doing, experience
Divine connection with Me.

Jesus is your brother
and he took human form
that you may
identify with his humanness
and see him as like yourself;
not God incarnate as
the one and only Jesus;
but God incarnate as
every one of you;
as every human.

Therefore, you come to Me
and know Me
by first acknowledging
the Christ-likeness in yourself.
For, in knowing this,
you open the door to realizing your

blessing and connection with Me.
Step across the threshold
and you will never want to return
to the days when you
did not know.
Your humanness does not prevent
you from Divine connection.
It links you to Me
and merely presents as an
illusion of separateness from Spirit.

Christ shattered that illusion
so you all could see clearly
the reality of the nature
of My relationship with you.

I love you as I love Jesus.
You hold as much potential
as he actualized.
And I talk to you
as I talk to him.
There is no difference between you;
only similarity.
See that of Christ in yourself
and you will know
the strength and nature
of My bond with you.

Shifting

See Jesus as a representation;
not of God,
but of yourself
and what can be accomplished
through the awareness
of true connection and co-creation
with Me.
This is Christ in you.
It is more a redefinition of Christ;
not as Jesus,
but, as Spirit's indwelling presence
in every person.
When you know this,
you know yourself as *yourself*
and you relate to Me
in your own special personal way
and we have a real relationship
Based on Who you are.

Joelle Mueller

The Real Rock

Stand in the middle of it
as it swirls around
like oily colors on water.
It is all illusion
and you are the only thing
to which you can cling.
Only you is real.
So, be the Real you
and become a rock in the pond.
and let the swirling masses
see that they can be
their own rocks…
their own Real selves.

You are it

You know your Real self is Me,
just as every other person's
real self is Me.
So, if I Am you
and I Am every other person,
you are every person
and every *other* is you.
For, as I Am one with you and all,
you and all are one with me.
Hence, you are one with each other.
And if you are all one,
there is only one,
and that one is you.
You are one.
Every other person is one.
I Am one.
We are one.
We are it.
We are all.
We are.

Joelle Mueller

You got it

Whisper to me, God;
so I can hear You
in my ear.
Because, when I only hear
you in my head,
your words get mixed up
with my ego,
and I sometimes wonder
if I got the message
straight.

Neither closer nor farther

"I feel different, God;
like closer to you and yet,
somehow, farther away.
Why is that?
Where does that come from?"

You feel different
because you *are* different,
and yet, the same
as you have always been,
and you are becoming
your real self.

Joelle Mueller

Heart Bearer

You are neither here nor there;
Neither grown nor small.
Your life is springing in an
unstoppable direction
and you must go along
for the ride.

"When will I be grown?"

When you can reach
all the hearts on the tree.
Then you will be larger
than your life
and a creator and supporter
like the tree.
Love will run through you
like sap
and you will bear hearts
like leaves.

Again

Once again;
stand amidst the swirling
and feel yourself safe
and see yourself authentic,
as you remain still and apart
from this anxious
movement of change.
All is well.

Changing Tides

Transition flows into life
like trickling water.
It pools in the belly
and boils over
into the limbs,
where action can begin.
Be quiet and allow it
to percolate through your veins.
Feel the energy; the anxiety
that is flushing out.
When you have moved enough,
from where you were
you will, joyfully, find yourself
where you are.

Flutter Forth

Butterflies live in your soul.
Raise your consciousness
and let the beauty
flutter forth.

Very Good

You are wholly beautiful.
I created you complete.
Acknowledge and accept
all of you;
every part and every aspect
of you;
your darkness, your light,
your body, your personality,
your feelings, and foibles,
your mind, your spirit,
your sex and sexuality.
If you have issues
with any of these parts of yourself,
know that I bless them all.
I accept them all
and I love you.

Open All your Gifts

Your sexuality is a gift from Me.
Dance in it.
Revel in the things your body can do
and the sensations it reveals to you.
All loving is beautiful and blessed.
I created your body as it is
and I intend for you to discover
everything about it;
feel comfortable in it,
feel the passion in it;
let it come forth
and enjoy the ride.

The Next Big Thing

Please allow yourself
to feel sexual.
Please allow yourself
the sensations.
There is no shame in it.
There is only vulnerability.
And when you are vulnerable,
you dismiss the walls and veils
and you become available
to connect with Spirit,
and to connect with
the soul of your lover;
and you can decide to allow
both to work together
to open you to another level.

Remember & Live

Don't forget Who you are,
My lovely.
You have a new life in Me
and I want you to live it.
All within you is
without you.
Blessings flow like water
to your pool of thoughts.
Like a balm they cool
and soothe the pain
and wash you clean.
Your heart is pure
and your life reflects
your thoughts.
You desire happiness
and your life reflects it.
Embrace these new blessings
in this present
and find the blessings
in your pain.
Wrap your heart around it all
and call it good,
then live today
as if it were the only day
and love your way
toward tomorrow.

Truly See

Determining
a person's worth
by looking and deciding
is such a loss for you,
because, all you will see
is your own perception
masking the truth
of who that soul is.
So, you lose connection
with Spirit, genuine feeling,
and you lose connection
with yourself.
Drop that mask.
See beyond your perception.
See the person.
See the Life,
and you will live yours
more fully.

Be aware

Be aware of your expectations,
for they may lead you
where you do not need to go.

Expectations are ego-produced
by your insecurities and
loss of self-awareness.

Keep your eyes open
to the goodness that blesses you
and close them
to the "poor me" ranting
of your ego when
its impossible expectations
aren't met.

Thoughts

Love your spouse
by loving yourself.

. . .

Know yourself
by loving your spouse.

. . .

Know your spouse
by listening…
to what she says
and to what she doesn't.

. . .

Be kind to all
and you are kind
to yourself.

. . .

Live blissfully;
observe everything,
judge nothing,
and lend support
when there is a need.

Choose the Life

Bless it
and it returns to you in blessings.
Judge it
and it haunts your mind.
Forgive it
and it wanders away from you.
Rage against it
and it persists like a plague.
Respect it
and it loves you back.
Disdain it
and it darkens your eyes.
Love it
and it soars in your heart.
Hate it
and it turns your heart to stone.
Choose it
and it chooses you.
Let Wisdom guide your choices.

Joelle Mueller

Release and Be

You know Me
in your thoughts
and in the maturity
of your heart.
You see through My eyes
when you are
moved to tears,
and you feel
your Life wash
over you in waves
when you release
what you are holding onto.

Simultaneous existence

I do not leave you.
I cannot leave you.
That is an impossibility.
And, likewise,
you cannot walk away
from that which is
innately you.
Understand this—
There is no you
and there is no Me.
We, as One, are all
that exists.
Never fear My wrath
and abandonment.
That which is you
cannot abandon you.
You can close your ears to our Voice,
you can close your spiritual eyes
to the love that is offered you,
but that Love is still present
and enveloping,
even if you choose not to experience it.
Open your eyes and ears and heart
to the great symphony
we already are.
Play with Me.

Speak it

Your lover is
just as sensitive as you.
She is just as easily hurt.
She cries like you
when you can't see her
and she feels
the unsettled energy
in the air;
just as you do
when unspoken wonderings
linger in your minds.

Love her, talk with her,
and share your heart.
She is the one
you can most trust
to understand your heart;
and after you've broken through
the fear of being vulnerable
and bared your soul,
you need not fear losing her,
for she is the one
who will stay.

Set & Cast the broken

Stay here,
My lovely flower.
Bloom where
you are planted—
Keep moving because
you think you are wrong
by staying,
and you will
re-experience the things
you are now
running from;
when you stop to rest
long enough
in one spot.

Truth in Reality

You are a Spirit
to be reckoned with.
You are not your fear
and insecurities.
You need not worry
about how others think of you.
You need not worry about
rejection and abandonment.
For, indeed, when you worry
about it, you experience it
in your mind,
as if its already happened.
You create the thing
you fear,
by placing your energies there.

In reality, you cannot
be abandoned or rejected.
Love is ever-present in you.
It never leaves you.
Your dependence on
the love of others is what sets you up for hurt.
That is why...
you must,
love yourself first.

The Eclipse

Love does not show
itself in expectation.
Ego expects and judges
your worth and hers
and ego eclipses love
and causes it to suffer
in the lack of light.

Put away your ego
when love comes
and allow your differences
to bump against love's softness
so they may remain,
to add life
and evolution
to your lives.

Joelle Mueller

The Nature of Fear

i live
in the landscape of your mind.
i trickle
between cracks of knowledge
and permeate the cells of truth
with the opaque color
of fear.
i am your every doubt,
every panicked wondering.
i disable you
and churn in your guts.
i salivate
when your thoughts vibrate
in a frenzy,
and your body twitches
with dirty-nailed desperation.
i possess you.
You are mine.
i gorge myself
on your bile
and reproduce myself
from your panic.
i am Fear
and I will eat you whole.

Support

You do not have to walk
toward your destiny alone.
You have one with you
who believes in what you can do,
and who knows who you are.
Trust in her loyalty
and in her love for you.
She sees you in her future
and holds you steadfast
in her heart.

Joelle Mueller

Dropping Feathers

Soar toward your destiny
with outstretched arms
and let the fear and doubt
fall from you
like worn feathers—

They no longer serve you
and they can no longer
help you to your destination.
They will only slow
and detour you.
Shed what can no longer further you,
then fly freely
in the direction of your dreams.

Guess What?

...Your state of mind is your reality.

Joelle Mueller

Why Struggle?

Without struggle there is no change.
Without change there is no growth.
Without growth there is no living.
Without living, one dies.
You must struggle in life
to experience ultimate living.

Your Universe

Do not let your ears,
your limbs, your heart,
your thoughts, revolve
around the planet of your lover.
Your universe encompasses
many more planets.

Joelle Mueller

Are vs. Were

Your past does not
determine you.
You need not live
from the past.
You need not make choices
from perspectives rooted
in yesterday.
You need only live
this moment
and create yourself
choice by choice,
in this present.
Doing this, you realize
who you are,
rather than living from
who you were.

It is Time

Be still in thought,
My dear.
Good intentions and actions,
out of love,
are always right—
and, in the long run,
reap only truth for you.
Know yourself
and your desires
for the future.
All is well
and as is meant.
You are here, right now,
to learn what
you can no longer do
and to learn
what it is
you must do.
Please open your mind
and your heart to it,
and let it take you
to your destiny.

Joelle Mueller

About the Author

Joelle has written poetry since the age of 14. Individual poems have been published in <u>North Country</u> and <u>Peaceful Journeys; The International Library of Poetry</u>.

She is a lifetime seeker of truth and spent many years immersed in the sea of religion. She now chooses to nourish her spiritual self through various other forms of spiritual food.

Joelle believes *every* person is equal to every other, the same Spirit animates us all, and we *all* have the same potential to give and receive love and to manifest goodness in the world.

She knows this book can be a tool to accomplish that manifestation of Goodness by reminding us that we are not alone, we are One, and we ARE the Spiritual Self.